*This Precious Life*

# This Precious Life

## Encountering the Divine
## with Poetry and Prayer

ALDEN SOLOVY

*Foreword by Rabbi Leon Morris*

*CENTRAL CONFERENCE OF AMERICAN RABBIS*
*New York · 2021/5781*

LIBRARY OF CONGRESS CATALOGING-IN-PUBLICATION DATA
Names: Solovy, Alden T., 1957– author.
Title: This precious life : encountering the divine with poetry and prayer
   / Alden Solovy ; foreword by Rabbi Leon A. Morris.
Description: New York : CCAR Press, Central Conference of American Rabbis,
   [2021] | Summary: "Prayers, poetry, and meditations inspired by
   encounters with God. The first part draws from divine moments in our
   sacred texts, mostly the Torah but also the Prophets and the Writings.
   The second part focuses on sacred moments in our daily lives,
   connections with the Divine that occur simply because we are human
   beings created in God's image"—Provided by publisher.
Identifiers: LCCN 2020037852 (print) | LCCN 2020037853 (ebook) | ISBN
   9780881233681 (trade paperback) | ISBN 9780881233698 (ebook)
Subjects: LCSH: Judaism—Prayers and devotions. | Jewish meditations. |
   Jewish religious poetry, American. | Reform Judaism.
Classification: LCC BM665 .S565 2021 (print) | LCC BM665 (ebook) | DDC
   296.7/2—dc23
LC record available at https://lccn.loc.gov/2020037852
LC ebook record available at https://lccn.loc.gov/2020037853

Book interior designed and composed by Scott-Martin Kosofsky
at The Philidor Company, Rhinebeck, New York.

CCAR Press, 355 Lexington Avenue, New York, NY 10017
(212) 972-3636
www.ccarpress.org
Printed in U.S.A.
10 9 8 7 6 5 4 3 2 1

*For my all of my rabbis and teachers*
*—in particular, Rabbi Peter Knobel z"l—*
*who encouraged me*
*to explore my voice as a Jewish writer,*
*and Rabbi Hara Person,*
*my mentor and friend.*

# Contents

## Encountering God in Our World

# Foreword

*by Rabbi Leon Morris*

Iɴ ᴛʜᴇ Bᴀʙʏʟᴏɴɪᴀɴ Tᴀʟᴍᴜᴅ, *B'rachot* 26b, there's a discussion about the origins of praying three times a day. Rabbi Yosei son of Rabbi Chanina attributes the three daily prayer services to Abraham, Isaac, and Jacob, respectively. Each statutory time of prayer is based on a significant spiritual moment experienced by a particular patriarch. Abraham, who wakes up early in the morning to look out over Sodom the day after he prays on its behalf (Genesis 19:27), becomes the paradigm for *Shacharit*, the morning prayer service. Isaac, who went out to meditate in the field before evening (Genesis 24:63), is understood to have established *Minchah*, the afternoon service. Jacob, who happens upon "the place"—later, a Rabbinic euphemism for God—once the sun had set (Genesis 28:11) and, in falling asleep, dreams of a ladder connecting heaven and earth, is the one who establishes *Arvit*, the evening service. According to this early Rabbinic teaching, our fixed times of prayer originated in the spontaneous prayers of our Patriarchs. However, Rabbi Y'hoshua ben Levi brings to the Talmudic page a very different conceptual framework to serve as a basis for prayer. He maintains that the times of prayer were based on the daily sacrifices offered in the Temple in Jerusalem.

These two conceptual frameworks for prayer do not have to be mutually exclusive and could in fact be complementary. Their juxtaposition on a single page of the Talmud mirrors the necessary interplay between the fixed and disciplined nature of prayer on the one hand and the need for prayers to be *avodah shebalev*—the "service of the heart"—on the other. We need words that are shared by an entire community offered in prayer services that punctuate the day. But we also need prayers that resonate in our hearts and that express the inner life of the one who prays.

Much of Alden Solovy's liturgy occupies the space between these two conceptual frameworks. In his previous volume, *This Joyous Soul*, Alden takes a single word or phrase of the classic siddur and gives it new meaning, enabling us to hear it as we never have before. There, he combines the fixed and the spontaneous, the inherited words with innovative expression, in ways that touch the soul. Similarly, in *This Grateful Heart*, Alden composes words of original prayer for the established seasons and holidays of our calendar.

Here, in the first half of *This Precious Life*, the experience of our ancestors serves as the foundation for our own encounter with God. The position of Rabbi Yosei the son Rabbi Chanina is embraced and amplified. The lives of our forebearers have wisdom to offer us. Their experiences invite us in and serve as a basis for insight into our own lives. Those ancient stories inspire a creative impulse that fuels our contemporary hopes, dreams, and struggles.

Later in the same Talmudic tractate (Babylonian Talmud, *B'rachot* 31a), our matriarch Hannah is presented as another important model for the life of prayer. The Bible tells us that "Hannah spoke from her heart" (I Samuel 1:13). From her, the Talmud explains, we learn that we must direct our heart when we pray. True prayer must be intentional. It should not become rote or formulaic. In her spontaneity, Hannah coins a new way of speaking to God. Rabbi Elazar asserts that Hannah is the first person in the Hebrew Bible to refer to God as *Adonai Tz'vaot*, "Eternal of Heaven's Hosts" (I Samuel 1:11). Hannah's importance for later generations of Jews who read her story is less about being the mother of Samuel the prophet. For the Rabbis, Hannah models prayer that combines sincerity and creativity. In his trilogy, Alden Solovy provides the twenty-first-century seeker with new ways to speak about (and to) God that reflect our own reality.

Hannah is a model of prayer for another reason as well. Rabbi Elazar offers a second explanation for the verse cited above, "Hannah spoke from her heart": Hannah said before the Holy One of Blessing, "Master of the Universe, with all the hosts and hosts of creations that You created in Your world, is it so difficult in Your eyes to grant me one son?" In making her argument, Hannah invokes the parts of her body. She reminds God that her eyes are for seeing, her ears for hearing, her nose for smelling, her mouth for speaking, her hands for labor, her feet for walking, her breasts for nursing.

Hannah, for the Rabbis, grounds our life of prayer in the realities of daily living. Hannah's words of connection with God emerge from the struggles, disappointments, surprises, and joys that human beings inevitably face. In the second half of *This Precious Life*, Alden embodies the model Hannah provides—his words emerge from a life fully lived. Hannah finds the Divine in her daily struggles and ultimately in the sense that her prayers were fulfilled. Alden invites us to do the same.

Hannah's prayer is paradigmatic because it is expressed in her own voice. In *This Precious Life*, Alden Solovy once again offers us his unique voice and does so in a way that calls us to find our own and to offer it—and our very lives—as a gift and as a prayer.

# Acknowledgments

*God of creativity,*
*You have given me a grateful heart and a joyous soul,*
*And have blessed my life with the precious lives of*
*Those who have supported, helped, and encouraged me*
*As I pursue the call to write,*
*Sharing their wisdom and talents*
*In service to Your holy name.*
*You have sent teachers and counselors,*
*Friends and guides,*
*From all streams of Judaism*
*And from a myriad of faiths,*
*To travel with me on this journey of prayer and blessing.*
*May their enthusiasm return to them, tenfold,*
    *as gifts in their lives*
*And in the lives of those whom they love.*
*May their wisdom continue to echo into the world.*
*Bless these human sources of light*
*With Your abundant mercy and*
*Your manifold kindness,*
*Granting them health and happiness,*
*Joy and peace.*
*Amen.*

WHEN I WAS TEN YEARS OLD, perhaps twelve, I carried a *sefer Torah* for the first time. It was Simchat Torah. As I completed the circle around the sanctuary, the rabbi's wife asked me, "Isn't that heavy, Alden?" According to my mother, I responded, "No. It's not heavy. It's the

Torah." How could the Torah possibly be heavy? The Torah carries us.

My writing is carried by God and Torah, and by people who love God and teach Torah. It's carried by people dedicated to bringing into the world new prayers inspired by our *sifrei kodesh*, our holy books. It's carried by people exploring their own voices of prayer. My writing is carried by you.

The acknowledgments tell a book's backstory. The book itself is the main tale, of course, supported by insights from the author, known as the introduction, and by gleanings from a teacher, known as the foreword. Like the credits at the end of the movie, the acknowledgments tell us about the cast and crew behind the book, their roles, their influence, and how the book moved from the mind of the writer to the pages you hold in your hands.

Thanks to all of you who have supported my writing for more than a decade by reading, sharing, and commenting on my work online, by acquiring my books, and by using my writing in personal and communal prayer, sometimes in the most intimate and challenging moments of your lives. Thanks to those of you who've come to synagogues, gatherings, and virtual events to hear me speak, as well as those who've participated in my online teaching. You've made art from my writing, created music from my words, and have—literally—choreographed my words into dance. You've engraved my words onto headstones and have chanted them with haftarah trope. Your creativity inspires mine.

Here I focus on individuals who've had a direct influence on this volume: Rabbi Ruth Abusch-Madger, Asher Arbit, Rabbi Minna Bromberg, Mark Davids, Rav Mike Feuer, Tovah Leah Nachmani, Rabbi Meir Schweiger, and Haim Watzman. Pieces in this volume were also inspired by the

Rev. Dr. Martin Luther King Jr., Fr. Anthony de Mello, poet Maya Angelou, and poet Mary Oliver.

My writing is also carried by the love and support of my family. To my mother and sisters, thank you for your love and encouragement. To my daughters, Nikki and Dana, who are both writers, I cherish our conversations about writing, writers, and books. Your support and enthusiasm for my work means more to me than I can express here. I continue to be blessed by the memory of my wife, Ami *z"l*, who believed in my writing long before I did.

Thanks to the clergy, educators, synagogue directors, organizational leaders, and the leaders of online Jewish platforms who've given me opportunities to write and to teach throughout North America, in the United Kingdom, and in Israel. I'm particularly grateful for the partnerships that have evolved over the past few years, both with individual clergy and with your congregations.

Four amazing leaders and teachers read the manuscript and wrote beautiful messages of support. Thank you to Rabbi Andrea London, Rabbi Dr. Dalia Marx, Rabbi Ron Segal, and Rabbi Elaine Zecher for your heartfelt and generous endorsements.

Baked into this book is several years of deep learning at the Pardes Institute of Jewish Studies, Jerusalem. Thanks to all of my teachers. I've always had a Jewish heart and a Jewish soul; you've helped me cultivate a Jewish mind. Special thanks to the dean, Rabbi David Bernstein, and the president, Rabbi Leon A. Morris, for inviting me to serve as the institution's Liturgist in Residence.

Additional thanks go to Leon, my friend and teacher, who provided a beautiful and heartfelt foreword to this volume, teaching Torah in the process. As one of the editors of *Mishkan HaNefesh*, Leon has long been part of my CCAR Press journey, bringing my work into our *machzor*. Two years ago, Leon enthusiastically hosted the international book launch for *This Joyous Soul* in the Pardes *beit midrash* in Jerusalem. Leon, you have my deep gratitude.

Thanks to the CCAR Press Council for supporting this project. Special thanks to Rabbi Donald Goor, chair of the committee, who has been an advocate for my work from the beginning of my relationship with CCAR.

The artistic integrity of a book moves from the author, to the editors, then to the experts who craft the volume itself. Thanks to eagle-eyed copyeditor Debra Hirsch Corman, who has shown a deep and abiding dedication to all of the books in this series, as well as a strong feeling for the integrity of my work. Thanks also to Michelle Kwitkin for proofreading and Scott-Martin Kosofsky for design. Thanks to Barbara Leff for a stunning cover design that fits the final book in this trilogy.

With one exception, the Hebrew *chatimot*—the endings of several prayers—were crafted for this volume with the assistance of two dear friends. Thanks to Rabbi Myra Hovav for bringing knowledge of Torah and *Tanach* to the creation of the *chatimot*, and to Yael Schweid for her expertise with the *nikud*, the vowels.

After all that work, someone has to get the book out into the world. I'm blessed by the depth of commitment from the professional team at CCAR Press who have supported this enterprise. Thank you, Deborah Smilow, Tamar Anitai, Leta Cunningham, and Rabbi Dan Medwin. Special thanks to Raquel Fairweather for your ongoing enthusiasm and continual efforts in marketing and promoting all of our collaborations.

But I skipped a step, saving for last my deepest thanks to the three dedicated publishing professionals at the heart of this volume: editor Rabbi Sonja Keren Pilz, PhD, CCAR Press director Rafael Chaiken, and CCAR chief executive Rabbi Hara Person. All three had a hand in editing the book, which is a huge commitment of resources to such a small volume.

Skilled editors can take weak writing and make it strong. Their tricks are rewriting, editing, and sending the writer back to the page. These are reader-driven editors. There are also finesse editors—editors with an ear for the music of the words and the voice of the writer—editors who make writers sound more like themselves. These are writer-driven editors. Master editors do both, improving the text for the reader while bringing out the best of the writer's voice. This is a team of master editors.

Sonja, Rafael, and Hara are key players in the backstory of this book.

Truth be told, I cheated when I submitted the first draft of the manuscript. I included several pieces that I lifted from *This Grateful Heart* and *This Joyous Soul*, the first and second books in this trilogy. Rafael challenged me not to reuse pieces, even strong pieces that fit well with the themes. Between the first and second drafts of the book, I removed ten pieces—all the duplicates and two others that I decided didn't fit in the volume—and then wrote a baker's dozen as replacements, thirteen new pieces to fill out the manuscript. They are some of the best in this volume. Rafael would not let me rest on past work; he pushed for more.

One prayer that didn't hit the mark, "Sarah Imeinu," needed to be rewritten, but I wasn't sure where to take it. I was stuck. It looked like the best option would be to strike it, but Sonja didn't want me to give up on the piece. She offered to have a conversation together about the character of Sarah. On our call, as Sonja spoke about the complex life of our first matriarch, I began to rewrite the prayer, in real time. By the end of the call, we had the prayer you'll read in this book. More than that, my conversation with Sonja sparked the wave of writing that resulted in that baker's dozen of new prayers for this volume. It was one of those classic writer and editor talks that changes the course of a book.

The idea for this book was born at a circular table in the back of the Ben Ami coffeehouse on Emek Refaim in Jerusalem. The table near the dessert case. It's a place where Hara and I meet from time to time when she's here in Israel. Our brainstorming resulted in the concept for this book. As the new CCAR chief executive, Hara has more important projects than this one book. I'm profoundly blessed that she took time with this manuscript. She edits with the ear of a poet. Hara has been a coach, a mentor, my teacher, my rabbi, and my friend since we met. I'm honored to dedicate this book to her.

This book is also dedicated to Rabbi Peter Knobel z"l. Peter introduced me to Reform Judaism and welcomed our family into his congregation. He was the first of many rabbis who have encouraged me to explore my voice as a Jewish writer. His advice and wisdom continue to shape who I am as a liturgist. To Peter, to Hara, and to all of my rabbis, thank you.

Whenever I sit down to write the acknowledgments to a book, I wonder who I might forget, someone who influenced the story of this book that I inadvertently leave out. If that is you, please accept my apology. In reading this volume, you are now part of the story of the book. Thank you.

# Introduction

*Jerusalem, Nisan 10, 5780/April 4, 2020*

I'M SITTING AT MY DESK, sheltering in place due to the coronavirus. In fifty years, when the coronavirus is a distant memory, please God—or perhaps by then all disease will have been wiped off the globe—some readers won't know what I'm talking about. You do. Many of you, perhaps most, are doing the same thing in this precarious and surreal moment: protecting the preciousness of all human life—yours, your family's, your neighbor's—by drawing back from the world outside into the world within the walls of your own home.

The walls of my writing studio are covered with Jerusalem stone. My desk is a rickety home-office model, a put-it-together-yourself wood-simulation item purchased before IKEA was a thing. One wall of the study is lined with Jewish books, mostly siddurim, Torah commentaries, and other books of Jewish wisdom. Half of the bottom shelf is Hebrew-language books, a testament to my continued and only partially successful efforts to learn the holy tongue. The window faces east, my view through a tree-lined alley to a busy street that follows the 1949 armistice agreement line. The Old City is to the north. To pray, I swivel my chair ninety degrees to the left. The art on the wall behind me is Jewish, including a framed, hand-crocheted "Shalom" made by my Grandma Ida *z"l*, and a blessing for the home purchased too long ago to remember with my wife, Ami *z"l*. My window ledge is full of family photos. As of this moment, everyone is healthy. Let it stay that way.

Some of you may have been sick or seriously ill with coronavirus. Some of you might be ill even now as I write or will, God forbid, become ill soon. Others may be grieving the death of a friend, a family member, or dear one. Some of you are walking into harm's way to serve us: doctors, nurses, health-care professionals, police, fire, public safety, sanitation, food-chain workers, and more, all of the people in vital services. Each one of us is being asked—perhaps required—to consider what gives our lives meaning. What we value. Our connections. Our contributions. Our legacy. The past. The future. This very moment. This precious life. The place in which we encounter the Divine.

This is a book of prayers, poetry, and meditations inspired by divine encounters. The first half of the book draws from divine moments in our sacred texts, mostly Torah, but also the Prophets and the Writings. Written using a modern voice and a contemporary imagination, the text invites you to enter into these holy moments as experienced by our ancestors and to reclaim them as our own. The second half of the book focuses on holy moments in our daily lives, divine encounters that occur simply because we are human beings imbued with divinity. Divine encounters that occur because we've been given souls.

This book is a testimony to the preciousness of life. In the first half of the volume, you'll walk with God in the garden, calling out to Adam and Eve. You'll stand as witness to the moment of Creation, the Flood, the Tower of Babel, Jacob's ladder, and the Golden Calf. You'll hear the voices of Abraham, our father, and Sarah, our mother. You'll leave Egypt, dance with Miriam by the sea, build the Tabernacle, and experience prophecy. You'll encounter the Divine through experiences of our forebearers.

In the second half of the book, you'll also be asked—perhaps challenged—to experience the Divine in your daily life. You'll be asked to imagine flying between two horizons, step inside the light, and ride the river of life. You'll encounter spiritual vandals. You'll be asked to find the ethics in your eyes, the ethics in your hands, the ethics in your arms, and the ethics in your heart. You'll experience the Divine in the poetry of living.

*This Precious Life: Encountering the Divine with Poetry and Prayer* is the third book in a trilogy with *This Joyous Soul: A New Voice for Ancient Yearnings* and *This Grateful Heart: Psalms and Prayers for a New Day*. *This Grateful Heart* focuses on time and seasons, providing prayers and meditations for our days, both the holy and the mundane. *This Joyous Soul* turns to the siddur, the prayer book, offering alternative readings for our classic liturgy. *This Precious Life* examines divine encounters in sacred texts and in our daily lives. *This Precious Life* is intended for personal meditation and communal prayer, as well as religious and spiritual counseling. As a book of meditations, it offers depth and breadth of emotion. As a spiritual guide, it brings intimacy and tenderness, humility and gratitude, supported by a foundation of strength, faith, and hope.

My goal in writing *This Precious Life* is to open you, the reader, to experiencing deeply moments of divine encounter using the liturgist's hand and the poet's eye to illuminate holy connection, to help you uplift your prayers and sing in praise. Along with those lofty ideas, there are practical uses for this volume. Use these offerings in your daily prayers, in writing *divrei Torah*, and in learning about and discussing the weekly *parashah*. Clergy and Jewish educators might consider using them as part of adult, teen, and Hebrew school education, as well as in Torah classes, sermons, conversion programs, counseling with congregants, and interfaith dialogue. Most importantly, my hope is that you are inspired to write new prayers in your own voice, based on your experiences of the Divine.

From here, sitting at my desk in Jerusalem, sheltering in place due to the coronavirus, it's impossible to know what the state of the world—or the state of our worldview—will be when we return to the world or when you hold this book in your hands. What will happen to our trust, social interactions, the economy, our lives? How will we move through the world, day by day? How will the generation of children who sheltered at home be shaped by these precarious times?

This much is clear: this is a precious life. Your life. My life. Our lives. All precious. May we all live with a grateful heart and a joyous soul, sanctifying this precious life.

# Encountering God
# in Our Text

## *Before the Beginning*

From eternity,
From the place beyond the highest heavens,
Where stillness is motion
And motion is stillness,
Where nothing and everything meet,
Where time and timelessness are one,
God imagined a universe
In which existence
Could only begin
By first
Creating light.

וַיְהִי עֶרֶב וַיְהִי בֹקֶר, יוֹם אֶחָד.
*Vayhi erev vayhi voker, yom echad.*
And there was
Evening
And there was
Morning.
A first day.

## About the Heavens

Majestic Sovereign,
Artist of Creation,
Why did You put the stars
Beyond our grasp?
Was it Your desire
To keep us searching the heavens
For luminous spirals,
Shimmering clouds,
Rings of glorious light?
Was it Your plan
To summon us
To reach across the vastness,
To reach across the darkness and the distance,
With yearning and hope?
Or perhaps,
Once You created the canvas of sky,
Once You took out Your watercolors,
Your oils,
Your charcoals,
Your pencils,
Your palette,
You couldn't resist
The urge
To paint.

## About the Rainbow

Majestic Sovereign,
Source of beauty,
When did You decide
To create the rainbow?
Was this Your intention?
Or perhaps it was a
Fantastic discovery
The moment Your divine light
Burst through the firmament of heaven?
Did You know that
Your glory
Could be refracted
Through a simple lens of water?
Or were awe and wonder created
When You first saw
Your own colors,
When You first witnessed
Your own brilliant light
Arching across a deep blue sky?

## *Where Are You?*

Where are you,
My son?
Where are you,
My daughter?
Have you left Me
Alone
In the garden?

Or are you hiding
Because you cannot bear
The guilt
Of failing
Yourself
And me?

When I made you,
When the breath of God
Became the breath of life itself,
I didn't know
Quite how painful
Losing you
Could feel.

## The Next Garden

The garden must be overgrown by now
Without human caretakers
To tend the fertile beds.

What would we do differently now
If the gates of Eden opened
And we were readmitted to paradise?

## Marked

The day
You rejected my sacrifice
You marked me
As not good enough.

We are fragile souls
In fragile bodies,
Easily broken-hearted,
Easily broken.

My brother's blood
Cries out to me, too,
Even more than my yearning
For Your love.

## The Flood

The flood that tore
Through our lives
Rushed in without remorse,
Churning indiscriminate,
Random with wreckage.

We who survived
Gasped naked in the waters
Cold and alone.
We fought the raging sea.
We wrestled the torrent,
The wind,
The darkness,
And our aching hearts.

When the rain ceased
And calm eased in
We drifted on the water
Numb to radiant sunrises
And luminous skies.

Until, one day,
We began to swim east
Toward holiness
And the new dawn.
Weary, faint,
Nearly too tired to press on,
We looked up,
Exhausted,
And saw an ark
Floating gently on the horizon.

## Yearning to Return

We were fools
Attempting to build a tower
To the heavens,
Lusting for fame and power,
Lusting for godliness,
Lusting for the sky.

Our ancestors
Walked the garden,
And we still remembered—
The way children remember a story—
The fresh scent of the morning air
After Your presence
Passed among
The orchids and
The tulips and
The hollyhocks.

We were fools
Attempting to build a tower
To the heavens,
Yearning for peace and shelter,
Yearning for You,
Yearning for home.

We don't yearn to walk with You
In the garden anymore.
Perhaps
That is why
The gate is still shut.

## B'chol Lashon (In Every Tongue)

We sing praises
*B'chol lashon,*
In every tongue, in every voice,
In joy and sadness,
With enthusiasm and with love.

We seek truth
*B'chol lashon,*
In every tongue, with every breath,
In study and prayer,
With faith and with purpose.

We pursue justice
*B'chol lashon,*
In every tongue, in every land,
In word and deed,
With strength and with courage.

We study Torah
*B'chol lashon,*
In every tongue, in every generation,
In wonder and awe,
With zest and with zeal.

We are one people,
Present at Sinai,
Where God spoke
*B'chol lashon,*
In every tongue,
To every soul,
To every heart,
The whole House
Of Israel.

## *Let Go*

Let go.
Let it all go.
Let go of the darkness
That ties you to empty ideas.
Let go of the fear
That binds you to false gods.
Let go of the chains
That imprison you in foreign lands.
Follow God's voice
To an unseen horizon.
Follow God's command
To an unknown destination.
Surrender to the truth
That God summons you
To a sacred calling,
To Torah,
To mitzvot,
To healing the world.
Surrender to the wisdom
Of letting go,
Letting it all go,
So that glorious mystery
Will open before you,
So that life will become an adventure
In the palm of
God's hand.

## Avraham Avinu

Then, suddenly,
Like daybreak,
Clarity opened my eyes,
Righteousness opened my heart,
Truth opened my mind:
Stone figures are the works of human hands.
The heavenly spheres
The works of God's glory.
The one God,
The only God,
Invisible, indivisible,
Is the source of all.

Then, suddenly,
Like midday in the desert sun,
Light surrounded me,
Radiance and glory,
Awe and wonder,
The presence of eternity,
Calling me to wander,
Calling me to preach,
In the name of the one God,
The only God,
Invisible, indivisible,
The source of all.

Come with me
Fellow travelers,
Seekers of holiness and truth,
To the gates of mercy,
To the gates of faith,
Where we cast off the yoke of idolatry,

Where we worship,
Together,
The one God,
The only God,
Invisible, indivisible,
The source of all.

## Sarah Imeinu

Why should I be surprised
That you tied my son,
My only son,
To an altar?
That you could argue
For a city
But not for your own child?
After all,
You sold me as a wife
To other men,
Twice,
Sending me into the den of Pharaoh,
And the den of Abimelech,
To save your own life.

I am a matriarch,
Strong and unassailable.
Laughter is my shield and my dagger.
Here I am,
The mother of a nation,
The mother of a people,
A prophet of Israel.
Come with me
Fellow travelers,
Where faith and doubt meet,
In service to the one God,
The only God,
The source of all.

## Fire Within

My burns
Cannot be seen on my flesh.
They are in my lungs
And in my eyes.
What medicine will halt the smoldering,
The smoke that suffocates from within?

My cuts
Cannot be seen on my skin.
They are in my heart
And in my throat.
What medicine will heal the bleeding,
The tide that floods from within?

Ancient One,
Release me from the fire and the knife:
The flame that consumes hope and joy,
The blade that destroys time and seasons.

Holy One,
Rock and Shelter,
Your medicine is love.
Your salve is holiness.
Your balm is life.

בָּרוּךְ אַתָּה, יי,
אֵל רְפוּאָה וּמַרְפֵּא
מְקוֹר חַיִּים וְאַהֲבָה.
*Baruch atah, Adonai,*
*El r'fuah umarpei*
*M'kor chayim v'ahavah.*

Blessed are You, Adonai,
God of health and healing,
Source of life and love.

## Gather Me

Gather me unto my people,
The house of my ancestors,
The dwelling of our fathers and mothers,
The resting place of generations.

This is my comfort,
O my Rock,
This is my consolation,
O my Redeemer,
That my bones will not be left behind,
That I will be united with my forebearers,
To reside in Your embrace.

Gather me unto my people,
Unto my story,
Unto my legacy and my longing.
Let my heart and soul
Rest in peace.

## Who Walks So Near

God of mystery,
Who is this
Approaching my life
With radiance,
With beauty,
With joy and thanksgiving?

God of majesty,
Who is this
Who walks so near
To my yearning hand,
My tired eyes,
My beating heart?

Creator of redemption,
I give thanks for this gift of love
Whom You've directed
In Your secret ways
To enter my life.

Let us build a tent of compassion and delight.
Let us build a tent of kindness and service.
Let us build a tent of radiance and hope.
Let the generations gather in the shelter of our lives.
Let celebration resound throughout our days.
Let our lives become a blessing
To each other, our families, and our people.

בָּרוּךְ אַתָּה, יי, בּוֹרֵא הַחַיִּים,
הָרוֹפֵא לִשְׁבוּרֵי לֵב,
וּמְחַבֵּשׁ לְעַצְבוֹתָם בְּאַהֲבָה.

*Baruch atah, Adonai, borei hachayim,*
*Harofei lishvurei lev*
*Umchabeish l'atzvotam b'ahavah.*

Blessed are You, Adonai, Creator of life,
Who binds up sorrows with love.

## Bless Me

Bless me,
Dear father,
With wisdom and wonder,
So that I enter my life
With poise and pride.

Bless me,
Dear mother,
With insight and awareness,
So that I enter my years
With confidence and grace.

Bless me,
Dear children,
With laughter and joy,
So that I enter my days
With kindness and grace.

For your blessings are without match,
Your consecration without equal,
A rejoicing of your heart,
Resounding with compassion,
Echoing from generations past,
Echoing from the hopes and dreams of our ancestors.

Bless me,
And I will be blessed.
Bless me,
And I will bless others
With my heart and my faith,
My hope and my praise.

Let blessings from you
Pass through me
To heal the world.

Bless me,
And let us all be blessed.

## The Ladder

The ladder
Connecting heaven and earth
Is built of prayers and dreams.
It rests on wisdom and truth,
The solid foundation of Torah,
And it leans—beyond the sky and the clouds—
Gently against the courtyard
Of holiness and light,
A plaza leading to the
Gates of mercy, the
Gates of righteousness, the
Gates of wisdom, the
Gates of justice, the
Gates of repentance, the
Gates of forgiveness, the
Gates of tears, and the
Gates of prayer.

The ladder
Connecting heaven and earth
Is near,
So near.
If only you would turn to look,
To notice that holiness surrounds us,
To see the invitation to walk with God
In this life,
Exactly as you are,
Not an angel but
A human,
Carrying the breath of the Divine
Inside your heart.

## Demand Justice

Speak, sisters,
Speak up for fairness
And for truth.
Do not hope for justice—
Demand it.
Do not expect honor or integrity—
Demand it.
Claim what is yours,
With wisdom and cunning,
By right and by righteousness,
Perhaps even risking your life,
To become the mother
Of your own
Salvation.

## Plenty and Famine

When the famine began
We didn't believe it.
The world was ripe,
Overflowing,
Bursting with gifts,
And we took abundance
For granted.

When the famine ended
We didn't believe it.
The world was barren,
Withered,
A wasteland of emptiness,
And we took suffering
As given.

God of our ancestors,
You have given us the means to end hunger,
To defeat famine,
To bring bounty beyond measure
To all peoples, everywhere.

Grant us,
God of mercy,
The will and the wisdom
To let abundance flow.
So that each of us,
All nations,
Will share in Your gifts.

## Dear Brother, Dear Sister

How long,
Dear brother,
How long has it been
Since we saw each other?
Stood together?
Wept upon each other's necks?

How long,
Dear sister,
How long has it been
Since we embraced?
Shared stories?
Shed tears of joy and affection?

Come, let me hold you.
Come, let me hear you.
Come, let me see you.

Let this moment be for gladness.
Let this moment be for blessing.
Let this moment be for service.
Let this moment be for love.

בָּרוּךְ אַתָּה, יי,
הַמֵּשִׁיב לֵב אַחִים עַל אַחְיוֹתֵיהֶם,
וְלֵב אֲחָיוֹת עַל אֲחֵיהֶן.

*Baruch atah, Adonai,*
*Hameishiv lev achim al achyoteihem,*
*V'lev achayot al acheihen.*

Blessed are You, Adonai,
You turn the hearts of brothers to their sisters
And sisters to their brothers.

## When a New Pharaoh Arises

A psalm of memory,
When a new Pharaoh arises.
Do you remember how Pharaoh despised the children?
How he commanded that they be ripped from their
    mothers' arms and destroyed?
How he used babes to subjugate a people and undo a
    nation?
Do you remember how two brave midwives subverted
    Pharaoh's plans?
How arduous is the work of freedom!
For Pharaoh has a heart of stone,
And he hardens the hearts of all who serve him
With treachery and deceit,
With fear and disdain.
But you have a heart of flesh,
And the spirit of God's justice,
To lead like Moses and Miriam,
To serve like Aaron and Joshua,
To stand for righteousness like Shifra and Puah,
To unseat the reign of tyranny,
To wander the wilderness,
And to journey to a promised land.

## I Am Pharaoh

I am Pharaoh
When I willfully
Harden my heart
To beauty and holiness.

I am Pharaoh
When I willfully
Harden my heart
To love and tenderness.

I am Pharaoh
When I willfully
Ignore the call
Of the forgotten and oppressed.

Ancient One,
Open my heart
With joy and compassion.

I am like Moses
When I seek
The word of God
In the wilderness and on the mountain.

I am like Miriam
When I lead
Our people, rejoicing,
In celebration and song.

I am like Aaron
When I cleanse my heart,
To fulfill God's command
In awe and righteousness.

God who led us out of slavery,
Through the desert,
And into a new land:
Teach me to open my heart,

In loving service to You.
In loving service to Your Torah,
In loving service to Your people,
In loving service to Your Creation.

## The Work Unseen

Before my baby brother
Was the prophet of Israel,
God had already
Touched my eyes with vision.
I knew. I saw. I understood.
The tiny ark
Floating in the backwaters of the Nile
Held the future leader of our people.
Our hope of redemption.
In the reeds,
Unseen,
I waited to save him.

Do you think my stuttering brother
Could have written the Song at the Sea?
The ballad that our people would sing
As we crossed the Reed Sea?
The refrain that would be in our prayers
For eternity?
He led the people in my song.
When he was finished,
I took the women to a secret place
To celebrate our salvation by the hand of God.

We,
The sisters of Israel,
Do the work that chooses not to be seen.
We always have.
Like summoning water in the wilderness.
The work without which
The nation could not live,
Nor the story told.

## Crossing

Every journey of liberation
Crosses the sea,
Pursued by a vicious past,
Surrounded by fragile miracles,
On a steady march
To an unknown destination.

Every journey of liberation
Begins at midnight,
In the darkest hour of oppression,
With the blood of a sacrifice,
With secret signs
And anxious anticipation.

Let us sing a song of salvation.
A song of absolution, benevolence, and compassion,
Of deliverance, freedom, and emancipation,
Of power, rescue, and release,
Of pardon, restoration, and reprieve,
Of the might and the mercy of our Maker,
Of God's generosity and grace.

מִי כָמֹכָה בָּאֵלִם, יי!
מִי כָּמֹכָה נֶאְדָּר בַּקֹדֶשׁ,
נוֹרָא תְהִלֹּת עֹשֵׂה פֶלֶא!

*Mi chamochah ba-eilim, Adonai!*
*Mi kamochah, nedar bakodesh,*
*Nora t'hilot, oseih feleh!*
Who is like You, O God,
    among the gods that are worshiped?
Who is like You, majestic in holiness,
Awesome in splendor, working wonders?

Let every journey of liberation
End on the opposite shore,
Exhausted but jubilant,
On the edge of an undiscovered land,
With shouts of joy and delight,
When our struggle leads to redemption.

## Between Egypt and Sinai

Between Egypt
And Sinai
There is only the journey.
The long march from what was
To what might be,
From servitude
To service,
From pain
To purpose,
From Pharaoh
To God's holy mountain.

Some days,
More than I care to admit,
I am closer to Egypt than Sinai,
Closer to narrowness of mind
And constriction of heart.
Still, I see the mountain
And rededicate myself
To the destination.

Between Egypt
And Sinai
There is only one question:
Are we ready
To become a nation of priests,
Guided by Torah,
Serving God,
The Jewish people,
And all of humanity
With our hands,
With our souls,
And with our lives?

## Unknown Lands

So many unknown lands
Arise from the glorious earth.
So many undiscovered peaks
Rise from my beating heart.
This is the journey,
The place where we climb
Above the clouds,
The place where we enter
Our own wisdom and grace,
To see the sunrise,
To watch the sea shimmer
With morning light.
This is where
We meet our holiness,
Our love,
And our surrender.

God of Old,
Guide me through unknown lands,
The territory beneath my feet,
And the horizons that call my soul.
Let my passage be for righteousness.
Let my passage be for healing.
Let my passage be for wisdom
And for grace.

## Manna

Manna still flows from heaven,
Riding on beams of light,
Warmth and heat,
Awe and passion,
Wonder and glory,
Feeding this grateful heart.

Manna still flows from heaven,
Summoned with beams of prayer,
Mourning and jubilation,
Praise and thanksgiving,
Hope and yearning,
Praising God's holy name.

Manna still flows from heaven,
To sustain this land,
To nourish this soul,
To enliven the days
And bless the nights
With the bread of life
From the God of compassion.

## Dust and Water

I have tasted
The dust of my sins,
The grit of my misdeeds,
The sludge of bad thoughts
And wrong actions.

I have tasted
The pure water of goodness,
The font of my charity,
The clarity of good intentions
And generous acts.

God,
I am but flesh and blood,
Prone to error,
Inclined to holiness.
Guide me. Support me.
Lead me to a life of celebration.

Let the rivers of righteousness
Overflow their banks,
Washing clean the dust of sorrow,
Washing clean the dust of fear and misdeed.

My hands will do Your work,
My feet will follow Your path,
And my life will be a well
Of awe and wonder.

## Golden Calf

That day,
The day we stood
Before the mountain of God,
The day we stood
In the valley below,
When You seemed so distant
And we felt so alone,
We made a golden idol
And danced.

That day,
The day we shamed ourselves
And each other,
The day we forgot Your love
And Your promise,
When we made ourselves distant
And hid our hearts from You,
We made a golden idol
And danced.

How easy it is
For a heart to stray,
To worship false gods,
So many false gods:
Wealth and power,
Success and acclaim,
Passion and lust,
Beauty and comfort,
Substances and sex.
We make these idols
And dance before them.

God of forgiveness,
Let our hearts return to You,
Let our hearts cleave to You,
Let our souls yearn for You,
So that we shout Your praises,
So that we sing Your glory,
So that we dance before You,
All the days of our lives.

## Fleeting Moments

It was freezing
On the mountaintop
At night
When the silence
Crushed my body
Into the stone.

It was sizzling
On the mountaintop
At midday
When God's thunder
Grasped my mind
With terrible power.

Holiness leaves a mark
On the soul.
God's voice leaves a crack
In the heart.
There is no balm,
Only fleeting moments
Of solitude and stillness.

## Amalek Within

We remember
The day you set upon us from behind.
The day you attacked
The weak, the faint, the exhausted and defenseless.
We remember your savagery and glee,
Your malice and ruthless intent.
We remember the fear and the horror,
The shrieks and the cries.

Villain, coward,
Where do you hide?
Scattered among the nations?
Or have you quietly, secretly,
Infiltrated our lives,
Hardening our hearts to one another?
Children of Israel,
Banish Amalek from within,
So that he will be destroyed forever.

When we remember
To love and to cherish,
To build and preserve,
To walk in the ways of God,
Then this name,
This Amalek,
Will be blotted forever
From the face of the earth.
When we remember
The pain and suffering of others,
When we exile wickedness from our hearts,
Evil will disappear forever.

We will not forget.

## Be the Blessing

To be a blessing, to be a curse.
To speak with kindness, to speak in anger.
To act with compassion, to act with cruelty.
With a loving heart or with threatening hands.
To build. To destroy.
To lift up. To tear apart.
Mindful or thoughtless.
Careful or careless.
Openhanded. Closefisted.
Honest. Corrupt.
To strive for holiness, or to abandon God's word.

To be a blessing, to be a curse.
You gave us this choice, God of generations.
To bless ourselves, to curse ourselves.
To bless each other, to curse each other.
Let blessings pour forth from my life.
Let blessings rain down from heaven.

Be the blessing.
Be the blessing.
Be the blessing.

## Exodus, Again and Again

My father was a wandering Aramean,
My mother a wandering Jew,
Sent on a journey home,
The journey to a promised land.

His children's children were slaves,
And their children's children refugees,
History set in the journey from slavery to freedom,
A march repeated throughout the ages.

The Temple fell, it fell twice,
Our nation dispersed,
Yet we did not forget.
We have risen,
Again and again,
To dream of Jerusalem,
To yearn for Zion,
To pray for redemption in our own land.

My mother was expelled,
My father was pursued,
My children hunted,
Generations lost
To fire and knife.

We are a tide of survival,
Surging and receding,
Returning to our people,
Returning to our God,
Returning, once again, to our land.

We are home.
Exiled no more.
In prayer and repentance,
We are home.
In love and joyous yearning,
We are home.
We are home to stay.

Rock of Jacob,
Let peace descend on Zion and Israel,
And let gladness fill our hearts,
For the sake of Torah,
For the sake of Your children,
And for the sake of Your holy name.

## The Way Home

God of Old,
You led our ancestors to a land of promise,
A vision of abundance,
Milk and honey from holy soil.
Grant me the strength to follow that sacred path,
Trials in the desert,
Trials of the heart,
The journey home.

Ancient One,
Your voice resounds in the hills,
Your call echoes in the valleys,
Your mysteries waiting
In the desert and by the seas.

Home is in my breath,
In my eyes,
In my heart.
Home is in the joy and the laughter,
In the work and the struggle,
In the toil and in the rest.

בָּרוּךְ אַתָּה, יי,
אֱלֹהֵי אֲבוֹתֵינוּ וְאִמּוֹתֵינוּ,
הַמּוֹלִיכֵנוּ לְבֵיתֵנוּ בְּשָׁלוֹם.
*Baruch atah, Adonai,*
*Elohei avoteinu v'imoteinu,*
*Hamolicheinu l'veiteinu b'shalom.*

Blessed are You, Adonai,
God of our fathers and mothers,
You are the way home.

## Goodbye

When we watched you leave,
When we watched you walk away to die
In an unknown place,
With an unknown grave,
Alone with God,
We could not fathom
That for thousands of years
Our descendants
Would read these stories,
Still feeling the sorrow and loss,
Still wondering about the justice of your punishment.
We could not fathom
That for thousands of years
Our descendants
Would stay committed
To honoring and celebrating our journey
   in the wilderness,
Stay dedicated to learning and teaching,
Receiving and retelling,
The words that you wrote on a rock,
On a fiery mountaintop,
Alone with God.

## *Tabernacle*

Let me build Your Tabernacle
With my own hands
So that Your glory
Will dwell with us
Once again.

I will build a sanctuary
In the space between my heart and my soul,
Clearing the residue of sorrow and misdeeds,
Creating a place for Your covenant,
Your wisdom and Your truth,
To reside within me.

Come, my people,
Shake off your slumber.
Shake off your despair.
God's majesty waits only for an invitation.

Let your days be the woven fabric of love.
Let your life be the golden lamp of peace.
Together, we will become
The staves and the planks,
The walls, the curtain, and the table,
Each one of us a pillar,
A sacred congregation,
A faithful assembly,
In service to God's holy name.

## Salt and Honey

God of secrets,
Ancient whisper,
Music in wind,
Heartbeat in water,
Soul of eternity,
You are in my breath
And beyond my reach.
You kiss my eyelids
From beyond my sight.
You are pulse and rhythm.
The call of sunrise
At midnight.
The first star
And the last.

Let me bring salt and honey
To the tents of life,
To the tents of wonder,
To the tents of joy beyond understanding.
The salt that calls vitality.
The honey that calls love.
The salt that summons savor and essence.
The honey that summons heart and core.
Flavors of power and passion.
Flavors of holiness and rejoicing.
Flavors of yearning and desire.

Hear my prayer.
Let me be coarse and sweet,
Savory and tart.
A source of beauty,
A source of delight.

I will sing praises
To the unknown and unknowable,
The unseen and unseeable,
The untouched and untouchable,
The radiance that swirls around us,
The salt and the honey that flow from You.

## Fire and Ash

My love of God
Rises like savory smoke,
A sweet smell,
Ascending from the altar
Of my heart.

The fires burn.
Prayer. Healing.
Joy. Hope. Surrender.
Keep them burning.
Keep them alive and strong,
In the sanctuary of your heart.

Smoke will rise.
Ash will fall.

Let us carry these ashes
To a holy place.
They are the dust that remains
When we set our lives
Ablaze with joy and passion.

Tend the fires in your heart
With wisdom.
Give them power.
Let them breathe.
Make your life
A tabernacle of blessing.
Your life will be as incense
On the altar of God,
Sweet and savory,
With the scent of glory,
Leaving holy ash,
As a sign of your devotion.

## Stones of Remembrance

Whose names
Will you engrave upon your shoulders
When you stand before God in prayer?

Whose names
Will you carry in your heart
As you sing songs of blessing and praise?

God,
Remember us in the name of our ancestors:
Abraham and Sarah;
Rebecca and Isaac;
Leah, Jacob, and Rachel;
Moses, Miriam, and Aaron; and
_____.

[add names from biblical times who are meaningful to you]

God,
Remember us in the name of our sages:
Rabbi Meir, Rabbi Akiva, and Rabbi Nachman;
B'ruriah, Yalta, and Ima Shalom;
The Rambam and the Tur;
Rabbis Regina Jonas and Abraham Joshua Heschel; and
_____.

[add names of sages of the past who are meaningful to you]

God,
Remember us in the name of our teachers:
_____.

[add names of current scholars and teachers who have influenced you]

These are the stones of remembrance,
For the righteous and the driven,
The certain and the seeker,
The silent and the outspoken,
The steadfast and the heartbroken,
All who have led us,
Taught Your Torah,
And rallied congregations and assemblies
To Your service.

Let my name,
One day,
Be worthy.
Let my life
Become a tribute to Your wondrous works,
A remembrance of Your gifts throughout the generations.

## *Vows*

What vow can I make before You,
God of the ages?
What vow can I make before you,
My people?
Empty words sting the heart.
Empty promises rend the soul.

This is my pledge:
To love with all of my being,
To the best of my ability,
Even when love seems to have departed.
Yes, some days I will love
More deeply, more fully,
You, my God,
And you, my people.
Some days I will struggle
Even to love myself.
Yet here is my vow,
Simple and pure.
To remember that love surrounds us.
Not to give up
On love,
On loving,
On the love that flows from You,
On the love that surrounds us all.

## Take Me Apart

Take me apart,
Bone by bone,
Sinew by sinew,
Organ by organ,
To reveal the lesions and strange bumps,
The fungus and broken glass,
That blacken my veins,
That grind my joints,
That cloud my eyes.

I will take a knife and a wire brush
To scrape out the poison,
I will take rags and bleach
To wipe off the muck,
Until my heart glows
And my soul shines
With the fruit of my own labor.

Only then,
Holy One,
When my flesh shimmers
And my spirit soars,
Reassemble me into
The person
You intended
Me to become,
Clean and ready,
Holy and strong,
A sacred mirror,
Reflecting You
In Your vastness and glory.

## Blood on Holy Ground

We have all shed blood on holy ground—
Christians, Muslims, and Jews.
We have all used anger, violence, and hatred
To prosecute our cause.
Woe unto the land
That has soaked in so much blood.
Woe unto the generations
That have soaked in so much death.

We have all shed tears on holy ground—
Christians, Muslims, and Jews.
We have all buried the lost
And dressed the wounds
Of those who prosecuted our cause.
Woe unto the generations
Who have tasted so many tears.
Let no one proclaim innocence.
Let no one proclaim justice.
Let no one proclaim God's blessing.

We have all prayed for peace on holy ground—
Christians, Muslims, and Jews.
Bless the land
That has waited for our words to become deeds.
Let these hopes become the work of our hands.
Let these blessings become the work of our hearts.
Let no more blood be shed on holy ground.
Let all ground be holy.
And let peace spread to the four corners of the earth.

## *Tears, Too Close: A Prayer of Consolation*

These tears are too close to my eyes,
Ready to burst forth
For the sorrow that surrounds us.

These tears are too close to my heart,
Ready to burst forth
For the pain that surrounds us.

These tears are too close to my soul,
Ready to burst forth
For the heartbreak that surrounds us.

נַחֲמוּ נַחֲמוּ עַמִּי יֹאמַר אֱלֹהֵיכֶם,
כִּי נִחַם יי צִיּוֹן.

*Nachamu, nachamu ami, yomar Eloheichem,*
*Ki nicham Adonai Tziyon.*
Comfort, comfort My people, says your God,
For God will comfort Zion.

Well of compassion,
Comfort of generations,
Let us cry together
For all that has been lost,
And all that
Might have been.

אָנֹכִי אָנֹכִי הוּא מְנַחֶמְכֶם,
וְרַב שְׁלוֹם בָּנָיִךְ.

*Anochi anochi hu m'nachemchem,*
*V'rav sh'lom banayich.*
It is I, it is I who comforts you,
And great shall be your children's peace.

Yearning,
Still yearning,
For solace and consolation,

Yearning,
Still yearning,
With hope and faith,

Yearning,
Still yearning,
For healing to flow free.

קוּמִי אוֹרִי כִּי בָא אוֹרֵךְ,
כִּי הֶהָרִים יָמוּשׁוּ וְהַגְּבָעוֹת תְּמוּטֶינָה
וְחַסְדִּי מֵאִתֵּךְ לֹא יָמוּשׁ.
וּמַלְאַךְ פָּנָיו הוֹשִׁיעָם
בְּאַהֲבָתוֹ וּבְחֶמְלָתוֹ הוּא גְאָלָם.

*Kumi ori ki va oreich,*
*Ki heharim yamushu v'hag'vaot t'mutenah*
*V'chasdi mei-iteich lo yamush.*
*Umalach panav hoshiam*
*B'ahavato uv'chemlato hu g'alam.*

Arise, shine, for your light has dawned,
For mountains may move and hills be shaken
But My kindness shall not be removed from you.
And the angel of God delivered them,
In love and mercy God redeemed them.

## Is This the Fast?

*Peace, peace,*
*To those who are upright,*
*Those who are steady,*
*Those who bring holiness*
*And light into the world.*

Is this the fast that God desires?
To remember the homeless and the needy?
To bring healing into the streets
And justice into our courtyards?

Is this the sukkah we build?
To summon the hungry and forlorn?
To put food in the mouths of the poor
And bring strangers into our tents?

Is this the seder we host?
To end bondage in farm and factory?
To rally before the seats of power
In the name of the oppressed?

Is this the kashrut we keep?
To end mistreatment of flock and herd?
To live in harmony with the land
And use our resources wisely?

Is this the Torah we learn?
To hear the word of God,
With humility and delight?
To thirst for truth and yearn for wisdom?

Is this the Shabbat we observe?
To shake off the bonds of the mundane?
To restore our lives
And renew our dreams of the world-to-come?

Is this the prayer we pray?
To cry out to the Holy One in joy and sorrow,
In the name of wholeness and healing,
In the name of peace?

*Peace, peace,*
*In your gardens and in your groves,*
*In your houses and your villages,*
*For you will be called a delight,*
*A lamp of awe,*
*A beacon of wonder,*
*A source of healing,*
*And a well of inspiration,*
*Among your people Israel.*

## Take Us to the Mountain

Lead us to the river,
To cast our sins upon the waters.
The world may go mad;
We must stay sane.

Take us to the mountain,
To cast our eyes toward the heavens.
The world may go mad;
We must have hope.

יי, אוֹרִי וְיִשְׁעִי, מִמִּי אִירָא?
*Adonai, ori v'yishi, mimi ira?*
God is my light and my refuge secure,
Whom shall I fear?

Hate has come calling,
To consume the heart of justice,
To consume the heart of mercy,
To challenge our lives and our ideals.

יי מָעוֹז חַיַּי, מִמִּי אֶפְחָד?
*Adonai maoz chayai, mimi efchad?*
God is the stronghold of my life,
Of whom shall I be afraid?

Love, too, has come calling,
To enliven the heart of righteousness,
To enliven the heart of rejoicing,
To fulfill our hopes and our dreams.

We need not be prophets of doom,
To see that anger stalks the night
And threatens our days.

Arise, awaken,
Let us be prophets of blessing,
Let kindness be our message,
And *tikkun olam* the work of our hands.

Let us repent our own offenses.
Let us repair our own wrongs.
Let us be upright in our thoughts and deeds.

Fountain of Life,
Bring us to the river of Your blessings.
Lead us to the mountain of Your salvation.
Bring Your light to the nations.
Bring Your healing to the world.

אֶשָּׂא עֵינַי אֶל הֶהָרִים, מֵאַיִן יָבֹא עֶזְרִי?
עֶזְרִי מֵעִם יי, עֹשֵׂה שָׁמַיִם וָאָרֶץ.

*Esa einai el heharim, mei-ayin yavo ezri?*
*Ezri mei-im Adonai, oseih shamayim vaaretz.*
I lift my eyes to the mountains,
From where will my help come?
My help comes from the Eternal,
Maker of heaven and earth.

God of all,
Let Your *sukkat shalom*,
Your shelter of peace,
Descend from the highest heavens
To bless us and all of creation.

## Two Ravens

Two ravens
Flying over the hills
Can be
Messengers from God
If you look
With a prophet's eyes.

A fox
Scavenging in the Temple ruins
Can be
A sign of redemption
If you look
With a sage's eyes.

You Children of Israel,
Awake!
You are surrounded by mysteries,
Bathed in holiness,
The light bursting freely from ancient wisdom.
If only you would look with your heart.
If only you would see with your soul.
Then the secrets of gratitude and wonder
Would dance with you
Like wedding guests
Yearning for reunion
With God's holy word.

## Return Us to You

Open,
Gateway of holiness!
Open your mysteries and secrets
To a world yearning for truth.
Open your doors to Torah,
To sacred wisdom,
Invite the generations to enter.

עֵץ חַיִּים הִיא לַמַּחֲזִיקִים בָּהּ, וְתֹמְכֶיהָ מְאֻשָּׁר.
*Eitz chayim hi lamachazikim bah, v'tomcheha m'ushar.*
It is a tree of life for those who hold fast to it,
And all its supporters are happy.

For Torah is the keeper
Of ancient blessings,
Of timeless wisdom,
The foundation of faith,
The essence of One,
The rhythm of time,
The glory of our lives.

דְּרָכֶיהָ דַרְכֵי נֹעַם, וְכָל־נְתִיבוֹתֶיהָ שָׁלוֹם.
*D'racheha darchei no-am, v'chol n'tivoteha shalom.*
Its ways are ways of pleasantness, and all its paths are
peace.

Open,
Gateway of holiness!
The splendor of the beginning,
The radiance of the ending,
The way of our ancestors,
The doorway to our hearts.

הֲשִׁיבֵנוּ, יי, אֵלֶיךָ וְנָשׁוּבָה;
חַדֵּשׁ יָמֵינוּ כְּקֶדֶם.

*Hashiveinu, Adonai, eilecha v'nashuvah;*
*chadeish yameinu k'kedem.*

Return us to You, Adonai, so that we shall return;
renew our days as of old.

## Psalms

### *Abundance*

The heavens sing to the stars.
The stars whisper to the sun.
The sun caresses the sea.
The sea dances with the land.
The land shares its gifts,
For abundance fills creation
With energy and light,
And I breathe glory into my veins.

Cast your hearts to the rhythm of silence,
The pulse of eternity,
The wisdom of love,
The radiance surrounding us all.

Then the mountains will skip like rams once more,
The hills like young sheep.
The rivers will roar
And the sky will shimmer in the flow of bounty
    from God,
The Source of Creation.

Cast your fears to the wind,
Your doubts to the breeze,
Your losses to the earth,
Your regrets into the waters.
Open your hearts,
And let the heavens sing to you.

## Mountain Prayer at Twilight

This splendor,
This yearning of cliffs and crests,
This longing of ridges and heights,
This hint of eternity,
This poetry in rock,
Stretches from horizon to horizon,
Beyond the limits of this world.
Power. Thunder. Silence.

How glorious are the peaks at dusk?
How majestic at twilight?
וְתוֹעֲפֹת הָרִים לוֹ.
*V'to-afot harim lo.*
The heights of the mountains are God's.

I just want to do God's will.
God has allowed me to go up to the mountain.
And I've looked over.
And I've seen the Promised Land.

הֶהָרִים רָקְדוּ כְאֵילִים, גְּבָעוֹת כִּבְנֵי צֹאן.
*Heharim rakdu ch'eilim, g'vaot kivnei tzon.*
The mountains skipped like rams,
The hills like young sheep.
This beauty,
This echo of infinity,
This music of transcendence,
This steadfast power,
Summons us home.
מִלִּפְנֵי אָדוֹן, חוּלִי אָרֶץ.
*Milifnei Adon, chuli aretz.*
Tremble, earth, at the presence of God.

This twilight,
Let it be for shelter.
This coming daybreak,
Let it be for hope, for renewal, and for dedication.

יִשְׂאוּ הָרִים שָׁלוֹם לָעָם, וּגְבָעוֹת בִּצְדָקָה.
*Yisu harim shalom laam, ug'vaot bitzdakah.*
Let the mountains bear peace to the people,
And the hills, through righteousness.

## Cornerstone

Sisters of Israel,
How wondrous that your voices resound in our tents,
That your insights echo in our streets.
Your prayers have become our song.
The stone that the builders rejected has become
    our cornerstone.
The heart that the builders rejected has become
    our fountainhead.
The service that the builders rejected has become
    our foundation.
The wisdom that the builders rejected has become
    our teaching.

Rejoice and be glad.
Let the struggle continue
Until no one questions your birthright,
Until no one denies your place,
And your light frees us all.

Build a house of glory to God,
Build a house of praise to our Maker:
A house of prayer,
A house of song,
A house of Torah,
A house of truth.

God of our ancestors,
Bless the women who lead our people,
Rabbis and cantors, educators and activists,
Philanthropists and organizers, scholars and
  researchers,
Expanding our understanding and love of Torah.
Bless the work of their hands and the work of their hearts.

All Your works praise You,
Adonai our God,
And the righteous bless Your name.

## To Battle Injustice

*Happy are the ones who battle injustice,*
*For whom the world sings praises.*
*Happy are the ones who stand united,*
*Their voices become a trumpet of truth.*

A psalm of protest.
Admonish the ruler who misuses power.
Beset an evil government with judgment.
Call the people to the streets.
Dispatch the brave and the free in cries of protest.
Entreat the spirit of mercy.
Forge a sword of truth.
Grievance is your staff and
Honesty is your shield.
Injustice will shatter like pounded rock.
Joy and hope will sprout roots in its place.
Keep yourself true,
Let neither anger nor vengeance become your cause.
Make not an ally of violence,
Nor a friend of hatred.
Open your heart to all.
Protect the innocent,
Quiet the hearts of the victims,
Restore kindness to our nation.
Speak out, speak out.
Tomorrow rise to speak out, again,
Until all of us are free from tyranny,
Voices raised,
With power and purpose,
Your feet marching, praising, defending with
Zeal the zest of Creation.

*Happy are the ones who battle injustice.*
*For their hearts will be sanctified in heaven*
*And remembered on earth.*

## Secret Light

The light of God
Is not well hidden,
Not so secret
That we must battle
The forces of nature
Or armies of evil
To stand in its glow.

It's there,
Behind your eyes,
Pulsing from the hills,
Rising from the sands.
It's there,
Inside a spade of dirt,
Inside the caper bud
And the orchid blossom,
In the old folks
And the little ones.

The light of God
Is not well hidden.
It's far enough
That you must begin the journey,
Yet close enough
That you will surely find it.

## Praise, Praise

Hallelujah,
Celebrate God!

Praise with song,
Rejoice with dance,
Attest with word,
Inspire with deed,
Shout with joy,
Exclaim with awe.

Proclaim God's majesty,
Recall God's works,
Adore God's wonders,
In hymns of love,
Sanctifying God's blessings,
Eternal.

Celebrate God,
Hallelujah!

# Encountering God
## in Our World

❦

## THE DIVINE IN THE WORLD

### *One You*

Love
Is a bridge
To the moment of Creation,
The moment
When God's heart
Could no longer be contained,
When light exploded
In a big bang,
Creating billions and
Billions of stars,
Millions and
Millions of galaxies,
Planets, moons,
Solar systems without number,
And one,
Only one,
You.

Yes,
You are
The impossible
Yet here-you-are
Miracle of love.
The impossible
Yet here-you-are
Miracle of life.
The impossible
Yet here-you-are
Miracle of God's
Loving hand

And outstretched arm,
Created in the same instant that
Holiness, mercy, beauty, goodness,
Righteousness, and grace
Began to expand
Throughout the universe.

## Two Horizons

There are always at least two horizons,
The one upon which the sun sets,
And the one that proclaims God's majesty.

An arch of radiant glory,
Visible only to those who choose
To fly above the clouds,
Above the mundane,
Above the steady ticking of the clock,
To soar in silence and love.

The brilliance of forgiveness,
The wonder of gratitude,
The luminance of love,
All shine without fail,
From the horizon of earth,
To the horizon of heaven,
Reflected in your heartbeat
And in the well of your eyes,
Emanating from the soul of the universe.

## Tending Gardens

Wildflowers bloom,
A field of colors,
A meadow on a hillside,
Untamed and free,
Tended by the sun and the rain,
Gently painted by the will of the earth.

Another place of delight,
My garden blooms,
A blueprint from my heart,
Guided by my hand,
Tended with love and with affection,
Planted according to my design.

God of splendor,
Grant me the willingness to
Plant gardens
And the wisdom to leave
Other gardens to You.

Teach me the beauty of doing
And the glory of not doing.
Grant me the power to act
And the strength to refrain.

Let my will to create,
And my willingness to accept,
Find balance and harmony
In my heart and in my hands,

So that my doing,
And my not doing,
Serve Your will
And Your world.

## Fresh Delights

Life is a garden of fresh delights,
Blossoming with wonders,
Large and small.
The first bird of morning,
The fresh smells of dawn,
And the promise of awe and adventure.

Holy One,
Help me to see, to love, and to cherish
This harvest,
This bounty of gifts,
This flow of sights.
Let me feel the rushing river
Pulsing in my veins.

Let me know the sacred sunshine
In my beating heart.
Let me thank You and bless You,
God of Old,
For Your steadfast love,
Day by day.

Life is a garden of fresh delights,
Blossoming with praises
For Your holy name.

## All Is Well

In the hills and the valleys,
In the wind and the clouds,
In the rivers and the oceans,
All is well.

In the rain and the rapids,
In the storm and the gale,
In the tempest and the squall,
All is well.

Oh, to live in this music.
All is well.
Oh, to live in this song.
This loveliness.
This beauty.
This knowledge.
This dance.
This chill at dawn and
This breeze at dusk.
These endings. These beginnings.
All is well.

In my courage and my fear,
In my honor and my shame,
In my silence and my thunder.
The hawk and the owl,
The egret and the crane.
The updraft and the horizon.
The downdraft and the breaking sea.
Soaring, soaring.

All is well.

## Duet of Joy and Sorrow

When the beginning ends,
And the ending begins,
So that the beginning
Can begin again . . .

In the moment
That the flame jumps
From match to candle,
Extinguishing the match
To bring light
Until the light is gone . . .

From the first cry of birth,
To the last sigh of death,
This precious life
Sings a duet of joy and sorrow,
The song of living,
Sung to music from beyond,
Sung to the rhythm of the heavens,
And the beat of your heart.

Let this day be for song.
Let this day be for joy and laughter.
Let this day be for blessing.
Let us bind our days with holiness and love.

## I Sing

I sing because God made music,
To lift our hearts and souls
From the hollow depths of darkness
To the highest heights of heaven,
From the cold shadows of desire
To the gates of radiant hope.

I sing because God made music,
To mark the moments of wonder,
To sanctify the moments of sorrow,
To soothe, to comfort, to gladden,
To cradle us with infinite harmony,
To rock us with eternal love.

I sing because God made music,
To give our souls a trumpet,
To give our wisdom a tambourine,
To give our prayers a voice,
To make our lives a song,
The instruments of God's blessings.

## The Largest Prayer

How small is the largest prayer?
A breath. A word. A whisper.
How immense is the deepest yearning?
A world. A universe. An eternity.
Oh my soul,
Oh my longing,
Oh my heart,
Oh my being.

How dear is this glorious life?
How precious are your beautiful spirits?
God spoke, the world burst forth.
When you spoke, my life resounded.
Love and joy.
Hope and passion.
Wisdom and gratitude.
Mystery and adventure.

How small is the largest prayer?
A blink. A heartbeat. And forever.

## *Before Morning*

Before morning breaks,
Before the birds begin to sing,
As dawn approaches from beyond the horizon
And the deep quiet night prepares to depart,
Let the angels bless me.
Let their songs be an echo
In my yearning soul.

Before morning breaks,
Before the traffic builds,
As light approaches the waking day
And responsibilities prepare to arrive,
Let the love of life surround me,
And let joy flow
From my grateful heart.

God who created light,
Holy One who renews Creation,
Bless the coming day with Your majesty and love.
Bless the hours with Your kindness and grace.
Bless our moments with hope and healing.
Let our songs of praise rise before You,
And let peace descend from the highest heavens
To cover the earth.

## Leaving

I've already left
The moment that just was.
I've already taken in new sights,
New sounds,
The rhythm and motion around me.
The gray dusk.
The morning light.

What is this thing called leaving
That feels so much like a knife
That pierces my safety, my solace, my peace?
I am leaving, always leaving,
And the world is always leaving me
In the next gust of wind,
The next quiet night.

Oh, to live in this breath,
This joyous expanse of air and light.
This here.
This now.
This wonder and amazement,
This luminous pulse of being.
Let the world sigh,
Let the earth turn,
Let the currents flow,
Let the space for tomorrow
Open with awe and surrender.

## *Arriving*

I've already arrived
In the moment to come.
The yet-to-be opens before me
As a flow of gifts and blessings,
Wounds and losses,
Nights and days,
A steady stream of danger and wonder.
The blue-white sky.
The moonless night.

What is this thing called arriving
That feels so uncertain,
Unsteady,
Unknown,
And yet so full
Of promise and hope?
I am arriving, always arriving,
In the next shimmering sunrise,
The next afternoon shadow.

Oh, to live in this heartbeat,
This amazing pulse of earth and sea.
This place. This space.
This radiant sigh of being.
Let the world laugh,
The earth cry,
The seasons ebb and flow,
So that the space for now
Opens with gratitude and peace.

## Now

This is now.
Always now.
Now and now and now.
The arrivals and departures
That bring me here
And take me away
Are only dreams and memories,
Windows and smoky mirrors,
Distractions from the pulse of this moment.

What is this thing called now that always leaves,
That always arrives,
That changes and stays the same,
That is always present, ripe and waiting?
This is now.
Always now.
And the world is full of
Now and now and now.

Oh, to live in this life,
This wondrous river of gifts.
This being. This becoming.
This shimmering light of awe and thanksgiving.
Let the currents flow,
Let the tides shift,
Let the moon rise and set,
So that now stays vital, vibrant, and alive
With joy and grace.

## I Am Breathing

I am.
Breathing.
I am breathing.
A prayer runs through it.
A prayer of hope.
A prayer of love.
A prayer of wholeness and heart.

I am.
Hearing.
I am hearing.
A song runs through it.
A song of joy.
A song of wonder.
A song of thanks and praise.

I am.
Seeing.
I am seeing.
A light runs through it.
A light of hope.
A light of love.
A light of wisdom and grace.

I am.
Being.
I am being.
My life runs through it.
A life of mystery.
A life of awe and splendor.
A life exalting God's holy name.

## Inside the Light

A rainbow shines
Inside the light.
If you could be the dewdrop
You would forever see it.

Stillness waits
Inside the light.
If you could be the sky
You would forever feel it.

The sunrise dawns
Inside the light.
If you could be the horizon
You would forever find it.

Freedom flows
Inside the light.
If you could be the wind
You would forever ride it.

Beauty rises
Inside the light.
If you could be the sparrow
You would forever reach it.

Mystery pulses
Inside the light.
If you could be the wonder
You would forever know it.

Majesty reigns
Inside the light.
If you could be the wisdom
You would forever sense it.

Faith rests
Inside the light.
If you could be the eagle
You would forever hold it.

Your soul glows
Inside the light.
If you could be yourself
You would never leave it.

## *The Cut That Heals*

What if I opened my heart
Fully, completely,
Without fear or hesitation?
Would I overflow with joy,
With beauty, with love?

Yes, my child,
You would overflow
With radiance and splendor,
With wonder and thanksgiving.

What if I opened my eyes
Fully, completely,
Without fear or hesitation?
Would I overflow with grief,
With loss, with desolation?

No, my child,
You would overflow
With kindness and grace,
With awe and compassion.

What if I opened my hands
Fully, completely,
Without fear or hesitation?
Would I drown in the work of repairing the world
In the depths of need and despair?

No, my child,
You would rise up
With strength and with wisdom,
A well of mercy,
A beacon of light at the gates of healing.

Remember this:
Love and loss are the same gift.
Grief and joy the same cloth.
Faith and doubt the same path.
The cut that wounds
Is the cut that heals.
When you rise up, renewed,
Tears and laughter will meet
In the core of your being.
Grace and mercy will flow through you
Like water.
You will be a fountain of blessings,
A source of righteousness and charity,
And you will sing humble praises—
Fully, completely,
Without fear or hesitation—
To God's holy name.

## You without Peace

You without peace,
Who yearn for God's blessings
But push them away,
Feeling their presence
And blocking their arrival,
Hoping for grace
Without gracing the hope
Of holy reunion,
Of blessings and wonder,
Know this:

Your heart is beautiful.
Your love is pure.
Your longing sings with truth.
Your journey is righteous,
Your path is lonely,
And God yearns for you
To keep searching
For the holiness and light
That surround us all.

## In My Distress

In my distress I call out
To You,
Holy One,
Who heals and loves,
And sometimes
Refrains.

What, then, is this prayer?
What, then, is my open heart?
I lay bare before You,
And You hold space for my grief,
For my sorrow and love,
For my confusion and wonder.

This life is a journey,
An uneven road,
Paved in light and shadow,
In darkness and daybreak,
So that when my footsteps falter,
I am drawn back to You.

In my distress I call out
To find the glory of holiness
I could not see,
The holiness that abandoned me,
The love I could
No longer find.

You who hears prayer,
Accept my tears as expiation,
As incense on
The altar of life,
As a guilt offering to
The ones I love.

Let my trust never fail,
Nor my hopes fade,
For You are
The source of healing.
The source of hope.
The source of faith.

In my distress I call out,
And my heart,
Still yearning,
Prays for rest.
Answer me.
Please, answer me.

בָּרוּךְ אַתָּה, יי, שׁוֹמֵעַ תְּפִילָה.
*Baruch atah, Adonai, shomei-a t'filah.*
Blessed are You, Adonai, who hears prayer.

## Spiritual Vandals

At the gates of an ancient city
A spiritual vandal cracked into my heart.
Stunned—expecting the blood of my grief and shame
To sizzle on the hot stone, ready to shout,
"How dare you touch that sacred place!"—
I saw a river of light flowing through me.
Starlight. Moonlight. Sunlight. Your light. My light.
Light from the moment of Creation.
So much radiance and glory.
Suddenly on my knees,
My forehead on the pilgrim's path,
I wept.

Now I wait at the gates
For you.
To invite you close,
To let me see the fissure in your heart
Ready to burst,
To touch it with love,
To crack you open
So that you can see the majesty
And the beauty
That flows through us all.

Listen,
Dear sisters, dear brothers:
Do not fear the vandals who guard
The gates of mercy.
For mercy is love,
And love is light,
And light seeks light,
And these angels only want to show
That it's been inside you
All along.

## A Human Journey

My soul needs a human journey.
Sometimes, I wish it weren't so.
Sometimes I wish that pain and suffering
Had no purpose and no meaning.
Or—if nothing else—God would
Share that purpose with me.
But, no, I must find that meaning
Myself.
Sickness and health.
Disaster and trauma.
The steady drumbeat of death
From the moment of birth.

My soul needs a human journey.
I embrace my fear
With an open heart.
I embrace my hope and my yearning,
Never knowing God's answers,
Releasing the vain notion that
God will show up to explain
How the foundations of earth were built.

My soul needs a human journey.
Here is where love resides.
Here is where I encounter you, my friends.
Here is where I encounter You, my God.

*Yah, Shechinah, M'kor HaChayim,*
Source of all,
Fountain of mystery,
Bless the hidden and the revealed.
Bless our moments and years.
Bless this human journey.

## Blessing Each Other

### Art and Practice

These are the practices of love
And the arts of peace.

Gratitude is the practice of sending blessings.
Compassion is the art of being a blessing.
Kindness is the practice of granting mercy.
Forgiveness is the art of being mercy.
Wonder is the practice of seeking holiness.
Humility is the art of being holiness.
Hope is the practice of seeing abundance.
Joy is the art of being abundance.

These are the practices of love
And the arts of peace.
Gifts of God
To share with each other.

## Show Me

Show me the works of your hands
And the deeds of your heart
And I will cause holiness
To pass through you
Like the wind through the trees
Summoning your soul
To mingle with Mine.

Set your mind to all
That is kind and just,
Compassionate and good.

Set your hand to all
That is right and true,
Charitable and healing.

Incline your heart to all
That is righteous and holy,
Glorious and full of wonder.

## Always This Wonder

Dear children,
Go outside to play—
In the sunshine and the breeze—
And we will bless your hearts,
Your precious laughter,
Your smiles and your freedom.

Run wild . . .
Skip . . .
Twirl . . .
And we will pray that you remember
Always this wonder.
Then, we'll remember our own
Carefree days,
Our own discovery,
Our own amazement,
Our own joyous hearts.
And you will bless us
With the secret and the power
To discover sacred wisdom
And the sea of happiness,
The sea of joy,
The sea of love,
Always this wonder,
Waiting within.

## Chop, Carry, Bake

We stand before
The hand of God,
The hand of earth and fire,
Of substance and mystery,
The hand of flour and water,
Of gifts and blessings,
The hand of life and death.

Open your hand to the needy
While you can,
Before your strength fades,
For you are called
To extend your heart in righteousness,
To extend your human hand in kindness,
To share your bounty and your labor,
In service to creation.

We stand before
The hand of God,
In awe and wonder,
To chop wood,
To carry water,
To bake bread,
To bring our blessings into the world
With love.

## Ethics

Strong and sure.
Gentle and soft.
The ethics of my hands.

Awake and bright.
Aware and kind.
The ethics of my eyes.

Brave and true.
Solid and steady.
The ethics of my legs.

Open and willing.
Able and ready.
The ethics of my arms.

Present and engaged.
Receiving and giving.
The ethics of my mind.

Joy and tears.
Comfort and hope.
The ethics of my heart.

## Rise on Wings: A Prayer of Borrowing

Let my soul rise
On the wings of your prayer.
My heart, heavy.
My voice, tired.
My strength, fleeting.
My breath, shallow.
My sight, obscured.

Your voice dazzles,
Filling the space with radiance and majesty.
A sacred melody.
A call of the ages.
An echo of eternity.
A pulse of holiness.
A harmony of light.

Let my yearning ascend
On the rhythm of your song.
Let my hope soar
On the music of your words.
Lend me your courage and your thunder.
And when we reach the gates of heaven,
I will be witness to your mercy and love.

## The Way of Spices

When you reach the way of spices,
Fiery and sweet,
Cinnamon and ginger, cumin and cardamom,
Inhale with all of your senses.
Taste this moment,
Mixtures of the familiar and the new,
Subtle and strong,
Salt and pepper,
The way of ending and beginning.

When you reach the path of color,
Bold and bright,
Azure and gold, crimson and amber,
Breathe the hues deep into your chest.
See this moment,
A palace of descending light,
Sparkling and radiant,
Brilliant and luminous,
The path of beauty and holiness.

When you reach the trail of shadows,
Dark and steep,
Unknown and meandering, shapeless and shifting,
Let courage guide your steps.
Ascend to this moment,
To this trail of victory and challenge,
Power and perseverance,
Bravery and honor,
The trail of wisdom and grace.

When you reach the road of fabrics,
Coarse and fine,
Burlap and silk, flax and silver threads,
Remove your gloves and shoes.
Feel this moment,
The tapestry we weave and reweave,
The seen and the unseen,
Stitched and embroidered,
The road of being and becoming.

When you reach the passage to your heart,
Delight in the grandeur,
Savor the brilliance,
And voyage into adventure.
Peace will be your companion,
And joy will be your guide.
Your nights will be bright with starlight,
And your days will shimmer with splendor.

## Recipe for a Life

1 cup gratitude
2 tablespoons humility
½ teaspoon pride
5 cloves love, 2 crushed
4 seeds forgiveness
2 tall stalks strength
1 tablespoon surrender
2 sprigs awe
3 shoots wonder
½ cup hard knocks, melted
1 cup fresh-squeezed joy
½ cup pounded sorrow
1 cup wisdom, sifted
1 gleaming ray of light
2 cubes compassion
Dash of fleeting time
Pinch of coarse suffering
Zest of music

1. Combine ingredients.
2. Stir with abandon.
3. Invite friends.
4. Sing.
5. Pray.

## Summon My Heart

There is no summit,
No peak,
No mountaintop
For me to find God.
God has already found me
In small moments and quiet breaths,
In the howling winds and the raging sky.

There is no road,
No trail,
No path
For me to find God.
God has already found me
In toil and in rest,
In the moonlit night and the glow at daybreak.

And yet,
God of Old,
You summon me
To wander and roam,
To journey, to discover.
To know You in all things.
To see You in all beings.
To love You with every breath.
To serve You with a full heart.

God of wisdom,
Grant me adventure and wonder,
Joy and amazement,
Seeking Your holy word,
Praising Your holy name.

## Give Love Wings

Give your love wings
To soar with the songs and the prayers
That dance between us,
That ring around us,
That rise shimmering
To the heavens
In radiance and glory.

Give your heart freedom
To float breathless
In the vastness of the universe,
To become one with the Soul of all being,
To enter the majesty of light
Pulsing from the ancient yearnings of our hearts.

Give your love wings, to soar.
And when you reach God's holy place,
Open your hands in blessing.

## On the Trail

God of beginnings,
God of mystery and adventure,
The path is steep,
The route is hidden,
The trail a narrow ridgeline,
Exposed and treacherous,
Slicing between majestic canyons,
Rising to the awesome sky.
The load is heavy, the destination unknown,
But the journey brings rhythm and dance,
Song and story,
Ancient music that rises around us,
To take us from sunset to sunset
As we move into the glorious unknown
Step by step,
Moment by moment,
Day by day by day.

God of the wayfarer,
God of the traveler and sojourner,
Divine light of wonder and truth,
Lead us.
Show us the way
Across vast open spaces
And through tight passages.
Guide us.
Show us the way
Through stormy days
And moonless nights.

בָּרוּךְ אַתָּה, יי,
נִשְׁמַת כָּל חַי,
הַשׁוֹמֵר צֵאתֵנוּ וּבוֹאֵנוּ,
מֵעַתָּה וְעַד עוֹלָם.

*Baruch atah, Adonai,*
*Nishmat kol chai,*
*Hashomeir tzeiteinu uvo-einu,*
*Mei-atah v'ad olam.*

Blessed are You, Adonai,
Soul of life,
Who guards our going out and coming in,
Now and forever.

## New Adventures

Every new adventure
Begins at the end of a trail,
Seen or unseen,
Physical, spiritual,
The place where going on
Makes no more sense,
The place where one more step
Would be a betrayal
Of every lesson learned along the way.

Every new adventure
Begins with a choice to enter the unknown,
To explore the wild and the majestic,
The sacred and the mundane,
To invite new moments
Of victory and challenge
Into our days,
To invite struggle and triumph
To walk beside us.

Every new adventure
Begins with faith in the journey,
Discovering the faith within us,
Finding faith in the daily blessings that
Surround us,
Guide us,
Carry us to
New vistas,
New horizons,
New landscapes,
Wonders beyond imagination.

## A Land Your Heart Knows

There is a land
That only your heart knows.
But if you trust the music in your veins
You will journey to the place
Where innocence and wonder
Merge inside your soul.
And you will emerge
Shimmering with light.

There is a dream
That only your eyes know.
But if you trust the music in the sky,
With love and surrender,
You will rise to the place
Where limits become possibilities,
Where endings become beginnings,
Where horizons flow toward you in the color of light.

There is a moment
That only your pulse knows.
But if you trust the music in the wind
And hear the secret of your breathing,
You will become a river of blessings,
A fountain of hope,
A well of healing,
And a source of peace.

## Seeking the One

Somewhere, in the middle of the ocean,
Unseen, unheard,
A white-capped wave breaks into one thousand seagulls
Soaring toward the sun,
To become a ray of warmth sent back to earth.

Somewhere, inside your heart,
Unseen, unheard,
A golden prayer breaks into one thousand sparks
Soaring toward the Soul,
To become a radiance of blessing sent back to earth.

You are the catalyst of holiness,
The alchemy of the Divine,
The wisdom that flows from God's river of light,
The hand that shares healing,
The heart that radiates love,
The seagull soaring toward the sun,
The spark soaring toward the Soul,
The one seeking the One,
Seeking the One,
Seeking the One.

## A Heart of Love

I cannot hold Your love in my arms.
I cannot touch Your presence with my hands.
Only my heart can know Your radiance and splendor,
Your compassion and forgiveness,
Your laughter and Your light.

Listen, dear sisters,
Dear brothers.
Do not be quick to pray
To embrace life from the center of your being,
To connect from the inside out.
When you hold love in the cradle of your heart,
You will drink at the oasis of joy.
But when sorrow dries up your aching chest,
You will be parched and faint
Before the fountain of God.

## A Heart of Vision

I cannot see truth with my eyes.
I cannot gain wisdom with my sight.
Only my heart can know
Your mystery and majesty,
Awe and wonder,
Glory and grace.

Listen, dear sisters,
Dear brothers!
Do not be quick to pray
For vision from the center of your being,
To see from the inside out.
When your heart pulses with joy and laughter,
You will rise weightless into the sky.
But when your heart cries its tears of blood,
You will be naked and alone in the arms of God.

## A Heart That Hears

I cannot hear Your voice with my ears.
I cannot touch Your glory with my hands.
Only my heart can know
Your justice and mercy,
Your law and command,
The deafening blast of Your shofar,
And the hushed whispers within.

Listen dear sisters,
Dear brothers!
Do not be quick to pray
To hear from the center of your being,
To perceive from the inside out.
When your heart beats with the music of the ages,
You will dance in the heavens.
But when silence empties your grieving heart,
You will lie vacant and hollow before the tent of God.

## A New Way of Being

This waking up
Is never easy,
When being asleep is so gentle,
So familiar,
So welcome,
And a new way of being
Is so hard to find,
So hard to live,
And so hard to keep.

Journey beyond the horizon,
Where joy and grace flow freely,
Where love is sacred medicine,
Where music sings and brilliance dances,
Where the arc of eternity bends to bless you.

This waking up
Is always surprising,
For being awake is so vital and vibrant,
A new way of being
Arising with ancient wisdom.

Come to a place
Where there is no more
Thirsty water or hungry bread,
No more heartless heartbeats,
Breathless breathing,
Vacant motion,
Or screaming silence.

Come to a place radiant with light illuminated
And life enlivened,
Where beauty glistens and awe shimmers,
Where the pulse of your soul
And the wonder of Creation
Beat with the rhythm of the universe.

## Faith to Pray

Grant me willingness,
God of Old,
To pray with my whole heart,
Knowing that You will not
Fulfill my every hope,
Nor change the nature of the universe
To suit my deepest desires.

Grant me faith,
God of compassion,
To pray with my entire soul,
Trusting that those prayers
Bring a measure of holiness into the world,
Whether or not I see it or feel it,
As surely as hatred and violence
Push holiness away.

Grant me courage,
God of mercy,
To pray with all of my might,
Turning those prayers into actions,
Using my strength in service to You,
So that my prayers become blessings,
And my days become a beacon of light and love.

## Fire and Water

One day
The fire of despair
Will sear your aching heart.
And when you wake
From this dream of death,
You will feel a vital new organ
Beating in your chest.

God of Old,
Let the fires of grief
Lift me toward You.

One day
The fire of love
Will sear your longing eyes.
And when you wake
From this dream of life,
You will see a vital new light
Shining from your face.

God of Old,
Let the fires of joy
Lift me toward You.

One day
The still waters of truth
Will soothe your yearning soul.
And when you enter God's word,
You will surrender to awe and majesty.
Holiness will fill your hands
With righteousness and charity.
Hope and peace will follow in your path,
And your life will shimmer with holiness.

DISCOVERY

## *The Pulse of Holiness*

The love
That echoes love
That whispers love
That breathes love
In the quiet stillness of morning
Is leading you toward light,
Toward understanding,
Toward God.
For love is the pulse of holiness,
The beating heart of radiance and wonder,
The rhythm of Creation,
The energy of blessing,
The starburst of the Divine.

Let love flow through you.
Let your countenance shine majesty
From the core of your being
To the edge of the universe,
To fill the world
With splendor.

The love
That echoes love,
That sings love
In your heart,
In the quiet nights of yearning,
Resonates with eternity,
Leading you toward light,
Toward the One,
Toward being one
With all beings,
With all souls,
With the wisdom of the ages,
And the wisdom of the earth.

## Rhythm and Grace

Let the music of your life guide you
And the rising sun warm you,
Bringing hope and laughter to your moments and breaths.

Let the power of your stance guard you
As the horizon blackens and the storm approaches,
Holding you firm and ready against the rising winds.

Let the wisdom of your heart ground you
When fear and doubt assail your footsteps,
So that you listen to the voice of love and truth.

Let the rhythm of your life grace you,
So that the spinning earth
Will carry you on a journey of joyous adventure.

## The Broken Sky

Look beyond the broken sky,
Cracked by a blaze of sorrow,
To the edge of the universe,
Where stars dance in endless spirals.

There is nothing as small as an angry mind,
And nothing so large as forgiveness.
There is nothing as wild as breathless love,
And nothing as free as your soul.

Look beyond the life you know,
Yearning for signs of truth,
To the gleaming edge of faith itself,
Where holiness sings to the willing heart.

## Dance in the Madness

Joy is a bird that lifts you in flight.
Prayer is a beacon that pierces the night.
Faith is a prism that opens the light.
God is the answer of joy and delight.

Fear comes calling, a poisonous art.
Judgment, a knife that cuts you apart.
Sorrow, a clamp that crushes the heart.
Loneliness threatens to never depart.

On this journey,
It's certain,
One thing is true,
Both joy and sorrow
Sit next to you.
So dance in the madness,
There is nothing new,
And love everyone
Who is dear to you.

## Renewal

Make for yourself
A quiet place,
Beyond the noise and chaos,
A place of refuge and retreat
To renew your mind.

Make for yourself
A prayer place,
Beyond the fear and doubt,
A place of comfort and calm
To renew your heart.

Make for yourself
A healing space,
Beyond the shadows and grief,
A place of hope and love
To renew your soul.

God,
Teach me to use my moments and days
As acts of renewal,
Drawing your divine energy
Into my life

So that I may serve You
And Your Creation
With the fullness of my being.

## Light, Overflowing

The light in me
Sees that the light in you
Is the light of God.

Oh brilliance!
Sparkling from your eyes.
Radiating from your chest.

Oh wonder!
Shining around us.
Sparkling with amazement.

Oh glory!
Overflowing my heart.
Touching your soul.

The light of God
Sees that the light in you
Is the light in me.

## Dance in the Sky

Let me dance in the sky,
With prayers and blessings
For the ones I love,
Raising these hopes
To the gates of heaven.

Let me sing among the stars,
With mystery and magic
For the holiness around us,
Raising these dreams
To the gates of redemption.

For there is music in the dawn,
And blessings at dusk,
A radiance of glory,
Carrying our voices beyond this world
To the One who created all being.

Source and Shelter,
You set the course of sun and moon,
Bringing on the evening twilight,
Calling forth time and space,
With majesty and wonder.

בָּרוּךְ אַתָּה, יי,
אוֹר שִׁמְךָ זוֹהֵר עַל פְּנֵי הַבְּרִיאָה.
*Baruch atah, Adonai,*
*Or shimcha zoheir al p'nei habriah.*
Blessed are You, Adonai,
The light of Your name shines throughout Creation.

## Wild Broken Heart

My heart is free,
Cracked open by fire,
Pouring radiance and music into the night,
Lifting prayers to the heavens.

This wild broken heart fears nothing,
Embracing stars and secrets.
What more can be rendered
Rubble and ash?
Dust and whispers?
My feet touch the hot core of the earth.
My hands reach the cold edge of the universe.
I am the hollow bone
That brings medicine and light
From the Soul of Eternity
To this world, to this life.

Take this wild broken heart,
Place it next to yours,
The wildness of your dreams,
The wildness of your laughter,
The wildness of your joy and love,
The truth that pulses through your veins,
And we will shine
Magnificent visions into the darkness,
Summoning the battered, the bruised, the wounded,
Summoning hearts split and torn,
Calling out to the thirst for healing
And the hunger to heal,
Calling wild broken hearts to the center,
To the place within where we all dwell.

Our wild broken hearts sing.
Our wild broken hearts bless.
Our wild broken hearts sparkle and shine.
Together,
Our wild broken hearts
Are whole.

# *Tanach* References

Return Us to You: Proverbs 3:17–18; Lamentations 5:21

PSALMS
Abundance: Psalm 114:4
Mountain Prayer at Twilight: Psalms 72:3, 95:4, 114:4, 7
Cornerstone: Psalm 118:22
To Battle Injustice: Psalms 84:4–5, 115:18, 144:15, 145:1–21
Secret Light: Psalm 97:11
Praise, Praise: Psalms 113–118, 136, 145–150

# Biographies

ALDEN SOLOVY spreads joy and excitement for prayer. An American Israeli liturgist, poet, author, and educator, he has written more than eight hundred pieces of new liturgy, offering a fresh new Jewish voice, often challenging the boundaries between prayer, poetry, meditation, personal growth, and storytelling. His writing was transformed by multiple tragedies, marked in 2009 by the sudden death of his wife from catastrophic brain injury. Solovy serves as the liturgist-in-residence for the Pardes Institute of Jewish Studies in Jerusalem, and his teaching spans from Hebrew Union College–Jewish Institute of Religion and the Conservative Yeshiva in Jerusalem to synagogues throughout North America, as well as Leo Baeck College in London and Limmud Conferences in the United States, Canada, and the United Kingdom. Solovy is the author of four books, two from CCAR Press: *This Joyous Soul: A New Voice for Ancient Yearnings* (2019) and *This Grateful Heart: Psalms and Prayers for a New Day* (2017). His work is anthologized in fifteen volumes from Jewish, Christian, and Catholic publishers, including the following CCAR Press editions: *Mishkan R'fuah: Where Healing Resides* (2012), *L'chol Z'man v'Eit: For Sacred Moments* (2015), *Mishkan HaNefesh: Machzor for the Days of Awe* (2015), *Gates of Shabbat: A Guide for Observing Shabbat* (revised edition, 2016), *Mishkan Aveilut: Where Grief Resides* (2019), and *Mishkan Ga'avah: Where Pride Dwells* (2020). He also writes for Ritualwell, RavBlog, ReformJudaism.org, and the *Times of Israel*. He is a three-time winner of the Peter

Lisagor Award for Exemplary Journalism. In 2012, Solovy made *aliyah* to Jerusalem. He is the founder of ManKind Project Israel. Find his latest work at www.ToBendLight. com.

RABBI LEON MORRIS is the president of the Pardes Institute of Jewish Studies. Rabbi Morris made *aliyah* with his wife, Dasee Berkowitz, and their three children in 2014 after serving as the rabbi of Temple Adas Israel in Sag Harbor, New York. He was the founding director of the Skirball Center for Adult Jewish Learning at Temple Emanu-El (now the Temple Emanu-El Streicker Center) in Manhattan. Ordained from Hebrew Union College–Jewish Institute of Religion in 1997, where he was a Wexner Graduate Fellow, Rabbi Morris has worked extensively with the Jewish community of India, beginning in 1990, when he served as a Jewish Service Corps volunteer for the American Jewish Joint Distribution Committee. He was also a Mandel Jerusalem Fellow. Rabbi Morris has taught at Orthodox, Conservative, and Reform institutions and is a regular contributor to the Jewish, US, and Israeli press. He is an editor of the new Reform High Holy Day *machzor, Mishkan HaNefesh*.

# Permissions

The following is reprinted with permission from *Haggadah Companion: Meditation and Readings* (Kavanot Press, 2014): "*B'chol Lashon.*"

The following are reprinted with permission from *Jewish Prayers of Hope and Healing* (Kavanot Press, 2013): "Dear Brother, Dear Sister" and "Gather Me."